CONTENTS

All The Way

Words by Sammy Cahn ❦ Music by James Van Heusen

Slowly

mp

mf

When some-bod-y loves you, it's no good un-less {he/she} loves you all the

way; Hap-py to be near you, when you need some-one to cheer you

all the way. Tall - er_____ than the tall - est tree is,

That's how it's got to feel; Deep - er_____ than the

deep blue sea is, that's how deep it goes___ if it's real.

5

Almost There

Words & Music by Jerry Keller & Gloria Shayne

me. We're al - most there, where we will share a

warm ca - ress, ten - der - ness, a dream come true for me, for

you. Love has wait - ed such a long time; now we're a kiss a -

part. Dar - ling, this is the right time to let the kiss - es

9

start. For_ you're_ al - most mine, and soon we'll

find our par - a - dise, par - a - dise so rare._

1.

Close your eyes for we're al - most there._

2.

there._

rall.

rall.

Ped.

10

AMAZING GRACE

Traditional

Moderato

1. A - maz - ing ___ grace! How sweet the sound that
(Verse 2 see block lyric)

saved a ___ wretch like me! _____ I

once _____ was __ lost, but now _____ am __ found; was

blind, but __ now I see. _____ 'Twas

grace that __ taught my heart to fear and grace my __

2. Through many dangers, toils and snares
   I have already come
   'Tis grace hath brought me safe thus far
   And grace will lead me home
   When we've been there ten thousand years
   Bright shining as the sun
   We've no less days to sing God's praise
   Then when we first begun.

AND I LOVE HER

Words & Music by John Lennon & Paul McCartney

1. I give her all ____ my love, ____
2. She gives me ev - 'ry - thing ____
3. Bright are the stars ____ that shine, ____

that's all I do. ____
and ten - der - ly. ____
dark is the sky. ____

And if you saw ____
The kiss my lov -
I know this love ____

my love ___
- er brings ___
of mine ___

you'd love her too. ___
she brings to me. ___
will nev - er die. ___

I ___ love ___
And I love ___
And I love ___

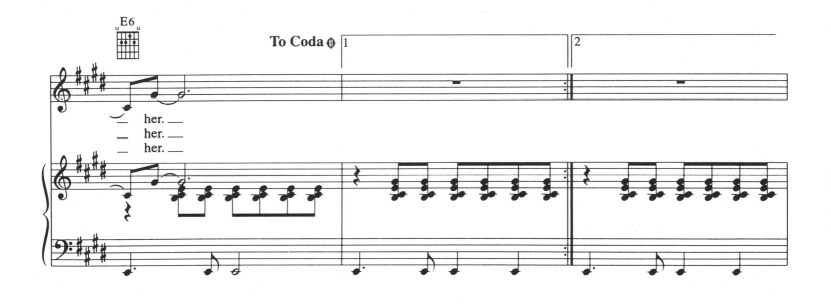

To Coda ⊕

her. ___
her. ___
her. ___

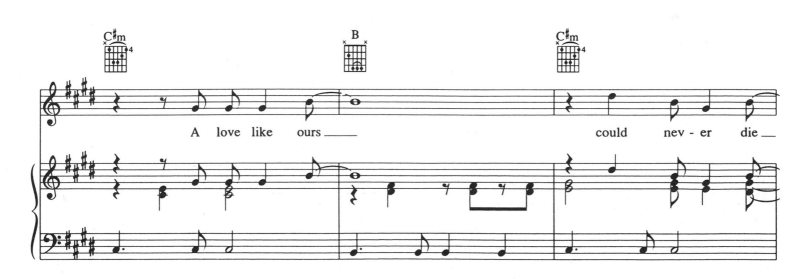

A love like ours ___

could nev - er die ___

will nev-er die.___ And I love___

her.___

17

Anniversary Song

Words & Music by Al Jolson & Saul Chaplin

said_____ The world_____ was in
on_____ Could we_____ but re -

bloom,_____ there were stars_____ in the
live_____ that were sweet mo - ment sub -

skies_____ Ex - cept_____ for the few_____
lime_____ We'd find_____ that our love_____

To next strain

__ that were there_____ in your eyes.
__ is un - al - tered by

time._____ Dear, as I held you so close in my arms,

An - gels were sing - ing a hymn to your charms

Two hearts gent - ly beat - ing were mur - mur - ing

low "My dar - ling, I love you so."_____ The

D.S. al Fine

A WHITER SHADE OF PALE

Words & Music by Keith Reid & Gary Brooker

23

As Time Goes By

Words & Music by Herman Hupfeld

And when two lov-ers woo, they still say "I love you," on
that you can re-ly;_____ no mat-ter what the fu-ture
brings as time goes by.
Moon-light and love__ songs, nev-er out of date. hearts__ full of pas-sion,

25

jeal-ous-y and hate; wo-man needs man and man must have his mate, that

no one can de - ny. It's still the same old sto-ry, a

fight for love and glo - ry, a case of do or die._____ The

world will al - ways wel-come lov - ers as time goes

27

Ave Maria

Composed by Franz Schubert

Original poem by Walter Scott ❧ German translation by Adam Storck ❧ English adaptation by Dr. Theo. Baker

A - ve Ma-ri - a! Maid - en
A - ve Ma-ri - a! Jung - frau
A - ve Ma-ri - a! gra - ti-a ple -

mild, Ah, lis - ten to a maid-en's prayer; For Thou canst hear a-mid the
mild, er - hö - re ei-ner Jungfrau Fle - hen, aus die - sem Fel-sen starr und
na, Ma-ri - a, gra-ti-a ple - na, Ma-ri - a, gra-ti-a ple-

wild,   'Tis Thou, 'tis Thou canst save a - mid _____ despair.   We
wild   *soll mein Ge-bet zu dir hin-we* — — *hen.*   *Wir*
na,   A - ve, _____ A - ve! Do - mi - nus,   Do - mi - nus te-cum.   Be-ne-

slum - ber safe-ly till the mor-row,   Tho' e'en by men out-cast, re-vil'd: O
schla - fen si - cher bis zum Mor-gen,   *ob Men - schen noch so grausam sind.*   *O*
di - cta tu in mu-li-e-ri-bus,   et be - ne - di - ctus,   et

Maid - en, see a maiden's sor - row,   O Moth - er, hear a suppliant child!
Jung - frau, sieh' der Jungfrau Sor-gen,   *o Mut - ter, hör' ein bit-tend Kind!*
be - ne - di - ctus fru - ctus ven-tris,   ven-tris tu - i, Je - sus.

fp   *pp*

A - - - ve Ma - ri - - - -
A - - - ve Ma - ri - - - -
A - - - ve Ma - ri - - - -

murk - y cav - ern's air so heav - y Shall
lä - chelst, Ro - sen - düf - te we - hen in
et in ho - ra_____ mor - tis, in

breathe of balm, if Thou hast smil'd; O Maid - en, hear a maiden pleading, O
die - ser dumpfen Fel - sen - kluft; o Mut - ter, hör' des Kin - des Fle - hen, o
ho - ra mor - tis no - stræ, in ho - ra mor - tis, mor - tis no - stræ, in

Moth - er, hear a suppliant child! A - ve Ma - ri -
Jung - frau, ei - ne Jungfrau ruft! A - ve Ma - ri -
ho - ra mor - tis no - stræ. A - ve Ma - ri -

a!
a!
a!

31

A - ve Ma - ri - a! Stain - less
A - ve Ma - ri - a! Rei - ne
A - ve Ma - ri - a! gra - ti - a ple -

styl'd! Each fiend of air or earth-ly es - sence, From this their wonted haunt ex -
Magd! Der Er - de und der Luft Dä - mo - nen, von dei - nes Au-ges Huld ver -
na, Ma - ri - a, gra - ti - a ple - na, Ma - ri - a, gra - ti - a ple -

il'd, Shall flee be-fore Thy ho - ly pres - ence! We
jagt, sie kön - nen hier nicht bei uns woh - nen! Wir
na. A - ve, A - ve! Do - mi - nus, Do - mi - nus tecum. Be - ne -

bow, be - neath our cares o'er - la - den, To
woll'n uns still dem Schick - sal beu - gen, da
di - cta tu in mu - li - e - ri - bus, et

thy   dear   guid-ance   rec - on-cil'd;   Then
uns   *dein*   *heil'- ger*   *Trost*   *an-weht;*   *du*
be -   - ne - di -   -   - ctus,   *et*

hear,   O Maid, a sim-ple maid-en,   And   for   a   fa - ther hear a child!
Jung-frau wol - le hold dich nei-gen   *dem Kind, das für den Va-ter fleht!*
be - ne - di - ctus fru-ctus ven-tris,   ventris tu - i, Je -   -   - sus.

fp   *pp*

A -   ve Ma - ri -   - a!
A -   *ve Ma - ri -*   - *a!*
A -   ve Ma - ri -   - a!

dim.

BRIDAL MARCH

Composed by Richard Wagner

Moderato con moto (♩ = c.104)

Chapel Of Love

Words & Music by Jeff Barry, Ellie Greenwich & Phil Spector

Spring is here, the _____ sky is blue, whoah, _____
Bells is will ring, the _____ sun will shine, whoah, _____

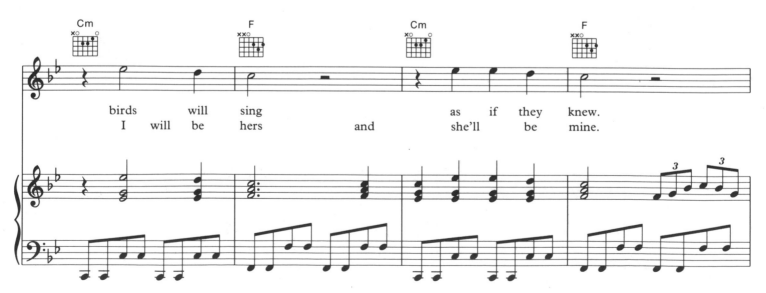

birds will sing as if they knew.
I will be hers and she'll be mine.

To - day's the day   we'll say I do,   and we'll
We'll love un - til   the end of time   and we'll

ne - ver   be   lone - ly   a - ny   more.

ne - ver   be   lone - ly   a - ny   more.   Be - cause we're

go - ing to the cha - pel and we're   going___ to get mar - ried,

go - ing to the cha - pel and we're   going___ to get mar - ried,

gee,___ I real-ly love you, and we're going___ to get mar - ried,

go - ing to the cha - pel of love.

Go - ing to the cha - pel and we're going__ to get mar - ried,

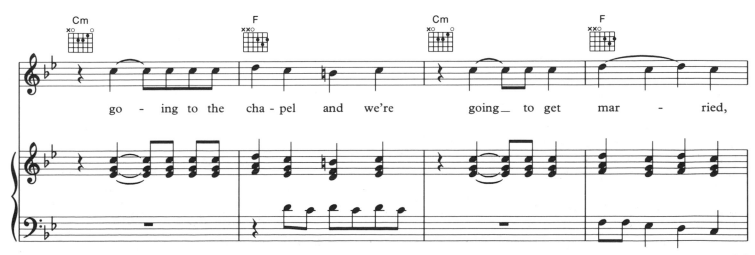

go - ing to the cha - pel and we're going__ to get mar - ried,

gee,__ I real-ly love you and we're going__ to get mar - ried,

go - ing to the cha - pel of love. Yeah yeah yeah.__

Go - ing to the cha - pel and we're going__ to get mar - ried,

go - ing to the cha - pel and we're going__ to get mar - ried,

gee,___ I real-ly love you and we're going___ to get mar - ried,

go - ing to the cha - pel of love. Be - cause we're

go - ing to the cha - pel of love, whoah whoah,_ we're

go - ing to the cha - pel of love.___

Could It Be Magic

Words & Music by Barry Manilow & Adrienne Anderson

der   of   all ___ of   you.   Ba - by   I want ___ you.
ic   at   last? _____

Tacet

D.%. al Coda

(Everything I Do) I Do It For You

Words by Bryan Adams & Robert John 'Mutt' Lange ♪ Music by Michael Kamen

Medium slow

1. Look in-to my eyes___ you will see___ what you mean to___
(Verse 2 see block lyric)

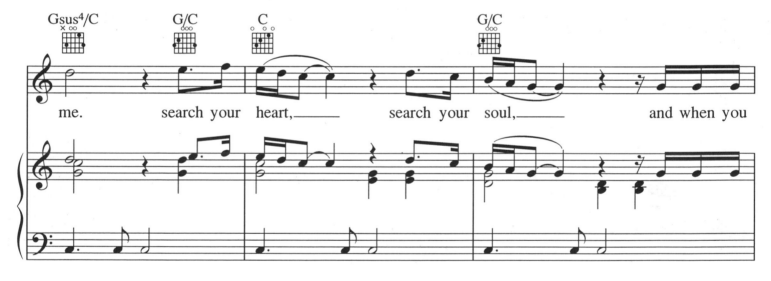

me. search your heart,___ search your soul,___ and when you

find me there you'll search___ no more. Don't tell me it's not worth try - in'

for,   you can't tell me it's not worth dy-in' for.   You know it's

true_____   ev-er-y-thing I do.   I do it for__ you.

There's no love   like   your love   and no

oth - er   could give more__ love,   there's no - where____ un -less

you're there all the time,_____ all the way yeah._____

Oh you can't tell me it's not worth try - in' for, I can't

help__ it, there's no-thin' I want more. Yeah__ I would fight for you,__ I'd

Verse 2:
Look into your heart
You will find there's nothin' there to hide.
Take me as I am, take my life;
I would give it all, I would sacrifice.

Don't tell me it's not worth fightin' for;
I can't help it, there's nothin' I want more.
You know it's true, everything I do
I do it for you.

COME LIVE YOUR LIFE WITH ME

Music by Nino Rota ◊ Words by Billy Meshel & Larry Kusik

No - - one can buy to - mor - row,____
Here, in our world to - geth - er,____

No - - one can sell their sor - row;____
Love will go on for ev - er;____

But,   when you look   in - to   my eyes,
Warm   in the shel - - ter   of   my arms,

Dar - ling, you'll al - - ways see_____
Dar - ling, you'll al - - ways be._____

Love,_____   I will give you   love;_____

Come   live your life   with   me._____

FINE

51

We'll have our good times, and ev - en in sad times, with love, we will find a way. No - thing else mat - ters but lov - ing each oth - er the way that we do to - day.

D.S. al Fine

52

FROM HERE TO ETERNITY

Words by Robert Wells ♪ Music by Fred Karger

FOR ONCE IN MY LIFE

Words by Ronald Miller ❧ Music by Orlando Murden

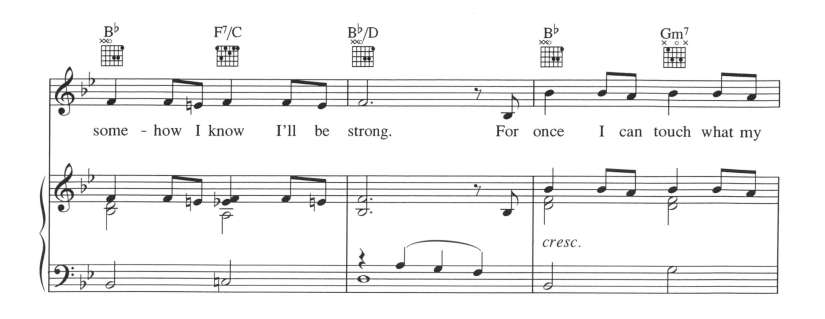

some - how I know I'll be strong. For once I can touch what my

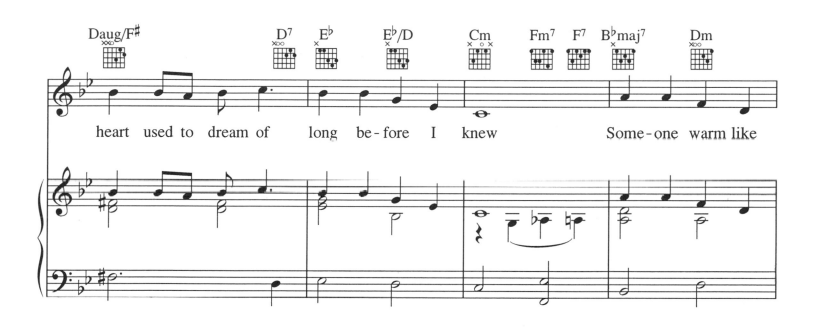

heart used to dream of long be-fore I knew Some-one warm like

you would make my dream come true. For once in my life I won't

let sor - row hurt me, not like it's hurt me be - fore. For

once I have some - thing I know won't de - sert me; I'm not a - lone an - y -

more. For once I can say this is mine, you can't take it;

poco a poco cresc.

1.

Long as I know I have love, I can make it. For once in my life I have

f

some-one who needs me. For once I can feel that some

bod-y's heard my plea; For

once in my life I have some-one who needs me.

poco a poco rit.

Get Me To The Church On Time

Music by Frederick Loewe & Words by Alan Jay Lerner

Brightly

I'm get-ting mar-ried in the morn-ing_____ Ding! dong! the bells are gon-na chime._____ Pull out the stop-per;

time!_____ If I am dan - cing,_____ Roll up the floor!_____

If I am whist - ling, (Whistle) me out the door!_____ For

I'm get - ting mar-ried in the morn - ing_____ Ding! dong! the

bells are gon-na chime._____ Kick up a rum-pus, But

don't lose the com-pass; And get me to the church. Get me to the

church. For Pete's sake, Get me to the church on time!

THE HAWAIIAN WEDDING SONG

Music & Original Hawaiian Lyric by Charles E. King ∮ English Lyric by by Al Hoffman & Dick Manning

Slowly, with much warmth

*Small notes for duet version with girl.

How Deep Is Your Love

Words & Music by Barry Gibb, Robin Gibb & Maurice Gibb

69

I real-ly mean to learn. 'Cause we're liv-ing in a world of fools,

break-ing us down when they all should let us be. We be-long to you and me.

D.%. to fade

How deep

I Love You Truly

Words & Music by Carrie Jacobs-Bond

Some - thing by your side to stand _____ Gone

is the sor - row, Gone doubt and fear, _____ For

you love me tru - ly, tru - ly, dear. _____

Coda

I love you tru - ly, tru - ly, dear. _____

rit.   *rall.*

I Love To Cry At Weddings

Words & Music by Cy Coleman & Dorothy Fields

Lyrics:
I Love To Cry At Wed-dings, how I Love To Cry At Wed-dings, I walk in-to a chap-el and get hap-pi-ly hys-ter-i-cal, The ush-ers and at-tend-ants, the fam-i-ly de-pen-dents, I see them and I start to sniff, have you an ex-tra

hand-ker-chief? And all through the serv-ice while the bride and groom look nerv-ous

Tears of joy are stream-ing down my face._____ I Love To Cry At
drink cham-pagne and sing "Sweet Ad - e - line."_____ I Love To Cry At

Wed-dings, an - y - bod-y's wed-ding an - y time! An-y-where, an-y
Wed-dings, an - y - bod-y's wed-ding just as

place._____ I long as it's not mine!_____

I Will Always Love You

Words & Music by Dolly Parton

Recite:
I hope that life treats you kind,
and I hope you have all that you ever dreamed of,
and I wish you joy and happiness,
but above all this, I wish you love.

Sing:
And I will always love you,
I will always love you,
I will always love you,
And I will always love you,
I will always love you,
I will always love you.

JUST THE TWO OF US

Words & Music by Ralph MacDonald, William Salter & Bill Withers

1. I see the cry-stal rain-drops fall, and the beau-ty of it
2. We look for love, no time for tears, wast-ed wa-ter all that
3. I hear the cry-stal rain-drops fall on the win-dow down the

all, is when the sun ___ comes shin-ing through. __
is, and it don't make ___ no flow-ers grow. __
hall and it be-comes ___ the morn-ing dew. __

To make those rain-bows in my mind, when I think of you some-
Good things might come to those who wait, not for those who wait too
And dar-lin' when the morn-ing comes and I see the morn-ing

Love And Marriage

Words by Sammy Cahn ♭ Music by James Van Heusen

Schottische tempo

Love and mar-riage, love and mar-riage,

Go to - ge - ther like a horse and car - riage, This I tell ya
It's an in - sti - tute your can't dis - par - age, ask the lo - cal

81

Love Is All Around

Words & Music by Reg Presley

and so the feel-ing grows.— It's writ-ten on the wind, it's ev-'ry-where I go,— so if you real-ly love me, come on and let it show.—

You know I love you, I al-ways will, my mind's made up by the

way that I feel. There's no be-gin-ning, there'll be no end, 'cause

on my love you can de-pend.

Repeat to fade

Verse 2:
I see your face before me
As I lay on my bed;
I cannot get to thinking
Of all the things you said.
You gave your promise to me
And I gave mine to you;
I need someone beside me
In everything I do.

LOVE ME TENDER

Words & Music by Elvis Presley & Vera Matson

EXTRA VERSE

4. When at last my dreams come true,

Darling, this I know:

Happiness will follow you

Everywhere you go.

LOVIN' YOU

Words & Music by Minnie Riperton & Richard Rudolph

Lov - -in' you_____ is ea - sy 'cause you're beau - ti - ful,

mak-in' love with you___ is all___ I wan-na do.___

Lov - in' you is more than just___ a dream come true,___

'cause ev - 'ry-thing that I do___ is out___ of lov - in' you.___

La la la la la la la la la la la la la la la la la___ la la___ la,

To Coda ⊕

doo doo din doo doo,— ah.—

CHORUS

No one else— can make— me feel— the co-lours that— you bring,—

stay with me— while we— grow old— and we— will live each day in spring-time;

{'cause lov - in' you——— has made my life— so beau - ti - ful,}
{'cause lov - in' you——— is ea - sy 'cause— you're beau - ti - ful,}

Makin' Whoopee

Music by Walter Donaldson ◈ Words by Gus Kahn

A lot of shoes,_____ a lot of rice,_____ the groom is ncr - vous,_____ he ans-wers twice._____ It's real - ly kill - ing_____ that he's so will - ing_____ to make whoop - ee!

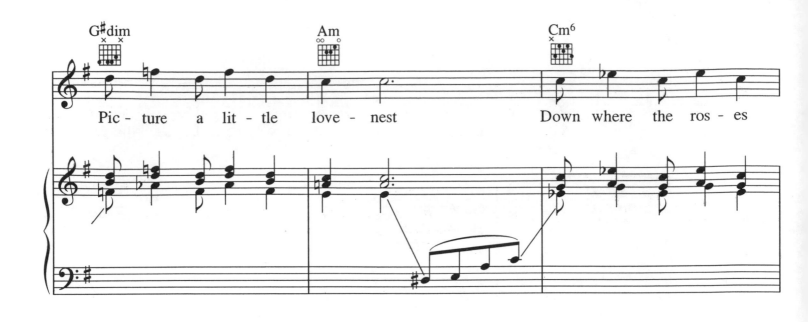

Pic - ture a lit - tle love - nest Down where the ros - es

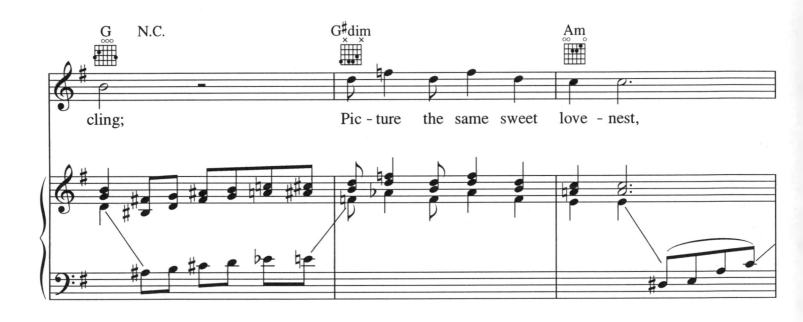

cling; Pic - ture the same sweet love - nest,

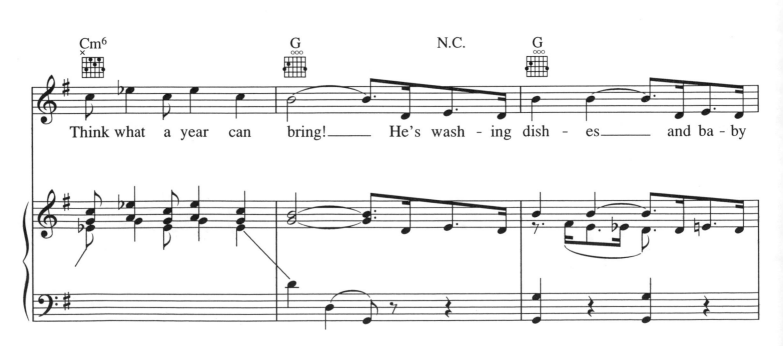

Think what a year can bring! He's wash - ing dish - es and ba - by

My Cherie Amour

Words & Music by Stevie Wonder, Henry Cosby & Sylvia Moy

2. In a cafe or sometimes on a crowded street,
   I've been near you but you never noticed me.
   My Cherie Amour, won't you tell me how could you ignore,
   That behind that little smile I wore,
   How I wish that you were mine.

3. Maybe someday you'll see my face among the crowd,
   Maybe someday I'll share your little distant cloud.
   Oh, Cherie Amour, pretty little one that I adore,
   You're the only girl my heart beats for,
   How I wish that you were mine.

More Than I Can Say

Words & Music by Sonny Curtis & Jerry Allison

Why must my life be filled with sor - row? _____ Oh, _____ love you more than I can

say.

Don't you know I need you so? _____

Tell me, please; I got - ta know. _____

Do you mean to make me

cry? _____

Am I just an - oth - er guy?

ONE HAND, ONE HEART

Music by Leonard Bernstein & Lyrics by Stephen Sondheim

On - ly death will part_____ us now._____

Make of our lives one life. Day af - ter day one

life. Now it be - gins, Now we start; One

hand,   one   heart.   Ev - - en   death   won't

part_____ us   now._____

now._____

One Moment In Time

Words & Music by Albert Hammond & John Bettis

heart - beat a - way   and the   ans - wers __ are all up __ to   me. __   Give __ me __

one   mo - ment __ in   time   when I'm   rac - ing __ with des - ti -

ny. __   Then   in that __ one   mo - ment __ in __ time,   I will

be,   I __ will   be,   I will be   free. __

I   will   be, I will be   free.

THE POWER OF LOVE

Words & Music by C. deRouge, G. Mende, J. Rush & S. Applegate

ly.   The feel-ing that I can't   go on

is light years a - way.   'Cause I am your la -

D. %: al Coda

cresc.

CODA

The pow-er of love,   The pow-er of love.

Repeat to fade

The pow - er of love.

SOMETHING

Words & Music by George Harrison

Some-thing in the way___ she knows___ And all___ I have___ to do___ is

think of her, Some-thing in___ the things___ she___ shows___ me. I

don't want to leave___ her now, You know I be - lieve___ and how.___

Speak Softly Love

Music by Nino Rota & Words by Larry Kusik

sky. The vows of love we make will live un - til we

die. My life is yours_____ and all be - cause You came in -

to my world with love so soft - ly, love. Speak soft - ly, love.

To Have And To Hold

Words & Music by John Worth

Some - day there's got to be___ a
watch - ing this love grow.___ I'll

heart that beats for me,___ I can hear it now. Too
take my time, al - though___ it's high time to live. Dis -

long to be a - lone,___ when some - one of my own seems a
cov - 'ring on the way___ that the price I had to pay I was

121

Unchained Melody

Words by Hy Zaret • Music by Alex North

Up Where We Belong

Words & Music by Jack Nitzsche, Will Jennings & Buffy Sainte Marie

far from the world we know; up where we clear winds blow.

clear winds blow. Time goes by,

no time to cry, life's you and I, a - live, to - day.

128

Take My Breath Away

Words by Tom Whitlock & Music by Giorgio Moroder

131

"Take my breath a - way."

To Coda ⊕

"Take my breath a -

way."

Through the hour-glass I saw ___ you. In time, ___ you slipped ___ a - way.

When the mir - ror crashed, I ___ called ___

___ you and turned ___ to hear ___ you say, ___ "If on - ly for to -

day _____ I ___ am un - a - fraid. _____

133

We've Only Just Begun

Words by Paul Williams & Music by Roger Nichols

We've On - ly Just Be - gun to
Be - fore the ris - ing sun we
And when the eve - ning comes we

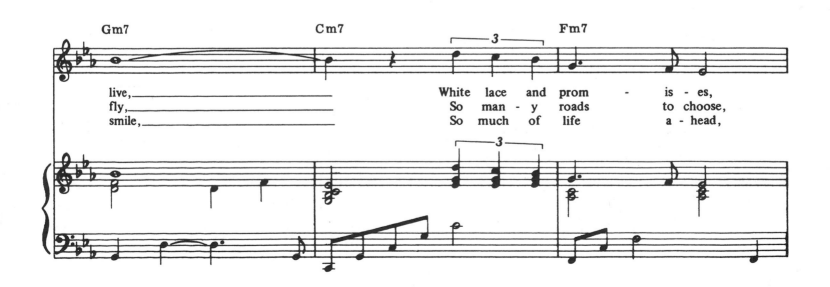

live,_____ White lace and prom - is - es,
fly,_____ So man - y roads to choose,
smile,_____ So much of life a - head,

THE WEDDING

Music by Joaquin Prieto ◊ English Lyrics by Fred Jay

You___ by my side, that's how I see___ us; I___ close my eyes, and I can see___ us. We're___ on our way to say "I do."___ My___ se-cret dreams have all come

day_____ you'll walk_____ down the aisle_____ with me._____ Let it

be,_____ make it be that I'm the one_____ for you;_____ I'd be

yours,_____ all___ yours, now and for - ev - - - er.

I_____ see us now, your hand in my hand. This_____ is the hour, this is the

140

141

WEDDING MARCH

Composed by Felix Mendelssohn

Allegro vivace ($\quarternote$ = 144)

143

THE WEDDING SAMBA

Words & Music by Abraham Ellstein, Allan Small & Joseph Liebowitz

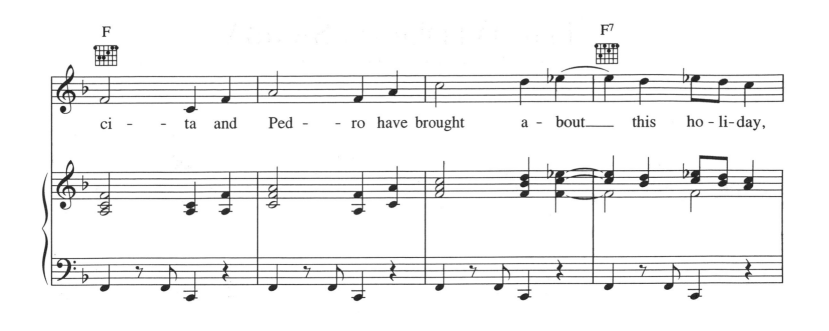

ci - ta and Ped - - ro have brought a - bout___ this ho - li - day,

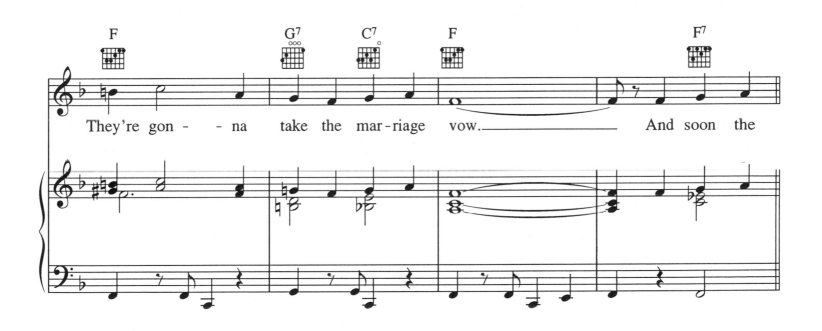

They're gon - - na take the mar - riage vow.___ And soon the

band___ will_ play a sam - ba,___ That's on - ly

145

goes on and hearts are so sub - lime._____ And

if you are not there to dance the Wed - ding Sam - ba

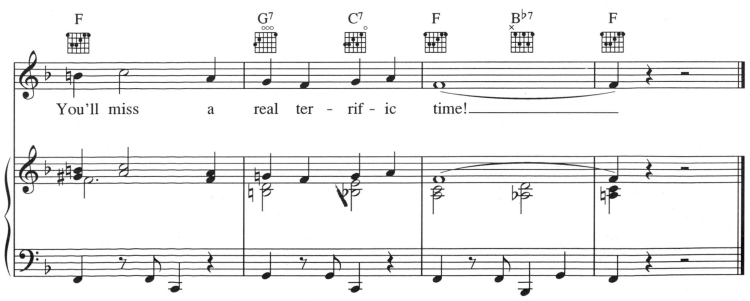

You'll miss a real ter - rif - ic time!_____

WHERE DO I BEGIN (THEME FROM LOVE STORY)

Music by Francis Lai & Words by Carl Sigman

1. Where do I be-gin_____ to tell the sto-ry of how great a love can be,_____
(Verses 2 & 3 see block lyric)

_____ The sweet love sto-ry that is old-er than the sea, The sim-ple truth a-bout the

songs,_____ with wild im - ag - in - ings. She fills my soul_____ with so much

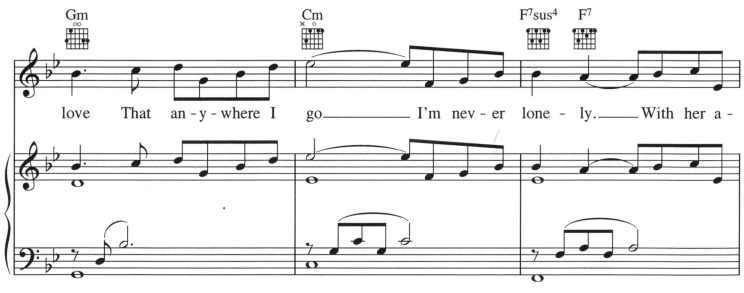

love That an - y - where I go_____ I'm nev - er lone - ly._____ With her a -

long,_____ who could be lone - ly?_____ I reach for her

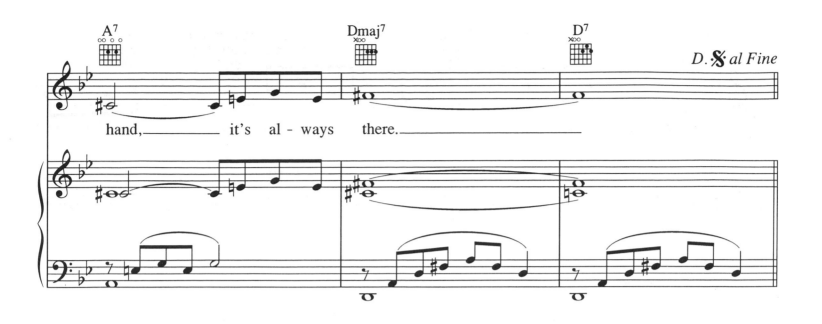

hand,_____ it's al - ways there._____

Verse 2:
With her first hello
She gave a meaning to this empty world of mine;
There'd never be another love, another time;
She came into my life and made the living fine.

Verse 3:
How long does it last?
Can love be measured by the hours in a day?
I have no answers now, but this much I can say:
I know I'll need her till the stars all burn away.

WONDERFUL TONIGHT

Words & Music by Eric Clapton

1. It's late in the eve - ning,
2. We go to a par - ty,
3. It's time to go home __ now,

she's won-d'ring what clothes __ to wear. __   She puts on her make-
and ev - 'ry - one turns __ to see __   this beau - ti - ful la -
and I've got an ach - ing head. __   So I give her the car __

D.%.al Coda

Coda

Oh, my dar-ling, you are

won-der-ful __ to-night." __

rit.

155

WHY AM I ALWAYS THE BRIDESMAID?

Words & Music by Lily Morris, Charles Collins & Fred W. Leigh

Why am I dressed in these beau - ti - ful clothes?

What is the mat - ter with me?

I've been the brides-maid for twen-ty-two brides,

This time -'ll make twen-ty - three!_____

Twen-ty-two la-dies I've helped off the shelf,

No doubt it seems a bit strange;____ ____

Be - ing the brides - maid is no good to me, And I

think I could do with a change.____

159

some fine day,_____

Oh let it be soon,_____ I shall

wake up_____ in the morn - - ing_____ on my

own_____ hon - ey - moon!_____

160